The Story of COALPORT CHINA WORKS

Ken Wilson

Series Editor Sheila Dunn

LANTHORN · LONDON

Coalport porcelain vase painted with view of Coalbrook Dale China Works. 55cm high. Now in Wells Collection Los Angeles County Museum of Art.

LANTHORN PUBLISHING LIMITED
  23 Greenwich High Road
  LONDON SE10 8JL

The Coalport China Museum comprises all that remains of a once flourishing enterprise on the banks of the River Severn. In these buildings thousands of people spent their working lives including children under eight years of age who worked a twelve hour day. Between them they created a world famous product, renowned for its style and quality. For 131 years, from 1795 to 1926, the firm survived good times and bad until it transferred to Stoke-on-Trent where it continues still to manufacture some of the original popular designs as part of the Wedgwood Group.

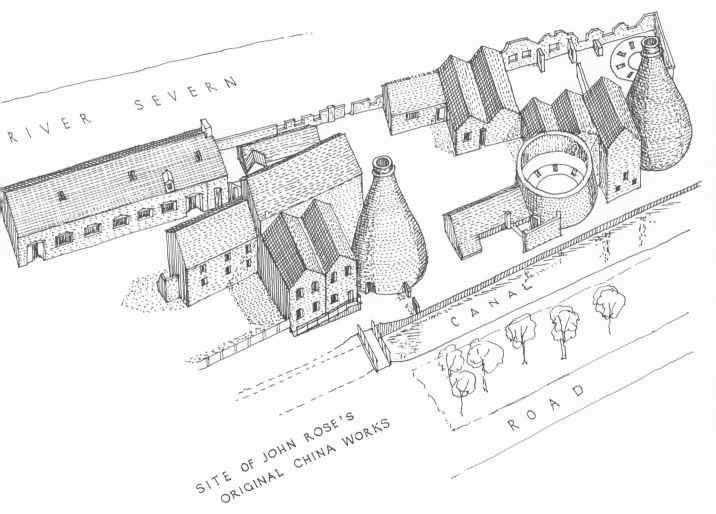

RIVER SEVERN

CANAL

ROAD

SITE OF JOHN ROSE'S ORIGINAL CHINA WORKS

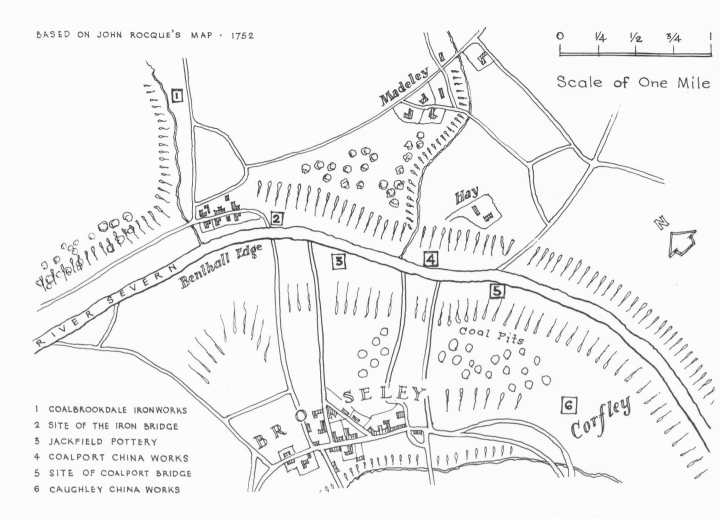

BASED ON JOHN ROCQUE'S MAP · 1752

Scale of One Mile

0   ¼   ½   ¾   1

Madeley

Hay

RIVER SEVERN

Benthall Edge

BROSELEY

Coal Pits

Corfley

N

1 COALBROOKDALE IRONWORKS
2 SITE OF THE IRON BRIDGE
3 JACKFIELD POTTERY
4 COALPORT CHINA WORKS
5 SITE OF COALPORT BRIDGE
6 CAUGHLEY CHINA WORKS

The Severn Gorge was beginning to respond to the Industrial Revolution by the middle
    of the 18th century but still retained its rural character. Broseley was then the
    largest village and the Coalbrookdale Ironworks was already of considerable size.
It would be another 27 years before Abraham Darby III spanned the river with the
world's first iron bridge. There was a pottery manufactory on the south side of the Severn
    at Caughley — then spelt differently — a modest building among the trees. Coal
was dug out of shallow open pits in the vicinity.

4

Thomas Turner was the son of a Rector of Little Comberton, near Worcester, where he spent his early years and possibly acquired an interest in the making of fine china which was produced in the area.

For a variety of reasons he was attracted to the Severn Gorge and to the earthenware factory at Caughley. This had been started by Squire Edward Browne on his Broseley estate and by 1754 was being managed by his nephew, Ambrose Gallimore. Coal was immediately available; there was also a superior clay to produce the saggars (thick earthenware boxes to protect the wares from damage in the kilns.)

Turner arrived in 1772 and was taken into the firm as a partner. In the same year the manufacture of soft paste porcelain was commenced. Caughley products were already highly regarded and the new lines increased this reputation still further.

Thomas Turner married Dorothy Gallimore in 1783 and became sole proprietor after his father-in-law's retirement. Four years later, at the age of 38, he travelled to France to study manufacturing processes and techniques. These researches enabled him to introduce within the next few years a range of products that would have a dramatic effect on the expansion of the business and would influence the future development of Coalport China.

Some acknowledge Thomas Turner to be the originator of the classic blue willow pattern, which is supposed to illustrate the story of a mandarin's eloping daughter and her lover changing into doves to escape capture.

After Thomas Turner's return from France a wide range of Oriental style designs were manufactured under the name "Willow Nankin" inspired by exported porcelain from China.

Thomas Minton worked at Caughley at the time and is credited in many references with engraving the Willow type designs. Later he joined Josiah Spode and subsequently founded his own firm.

CAUGHLEY IN THE 1790's

Raw materials and finished wares were delivered to and from the factory by boats on the river. The intervening distance to the wharves was covered by horses and carts over rough tracks or by men and women carrying baskets or panniers.

The Preen's Eddy Bridge was the first to cross the Gorge at Coalport. It was made of timber and opened in 1780. Nearby wharves, built at the same time, generated heavy use of the bridge. Piecemeal repairs kept the original design intact but there was severe damage in the floods of 1795 and it was finally replaced by an iron structure.

When the re-named Coalport Bridge was rebuilt by John Onions in 1818 it was similar in style to the first-ever cast-iron bridge, a mile and a half up-river, built in 1779 by the local iron master, Abraham Darby III, from components manufactured at his Coalbrookdale Works.

John Rose was born on 8 February 1772. He was the son of a Scot who moved into the Severn valley to farm. At the age of 12, John became an apprentice to Thomas Turner and was such an apt pupil that by the time he left, about 1790-91, he had almost as much skill and technical knowledge as his teacher.

Such was Rose's success that when his former employer retired due to bad health, about 1799, he was able to take over the Caughley business.

When John Rose first left Caughley, he went into partnership with Edward Blakeway, a successful draper, who had taken over one of the two modestly sized potteries at Jackfield. The business prospered and within a few years they were seeking larger production space.

In 1795, the partners were attracted to a site at Coalport. It was on the roadside, with the recently opened canal at the rear. On the other side of the canal was the earthenware manufactory of Bradley & Co which was owned by their new landlord, William Reynolds, and behind that was the river.

Blakeway & Rose's new factory was built on the principles of Wedgwood's proven and successful factory layout at Etruria in Staffordshire, which was a model for the industry. It was designed to accommodate the complete process of china manufacture.

William Reynolds was in the process of creating a new town at Coalport. He brought
  china manufacture, chain-making and boat building into the area and built new
  cottages for the workers they attracted. To facilitate transport of raw materials
  and finished goods he improved roads, built wharves and extended the Shropshire
  Canal. Reynolds was proud of his new development and watched the progress from
a cast iron gallery linking the two wings of his large house "The Tuckies" just
across the river.

An ironmaster first and foremost,
  William Reynolds was also an
  engineer, scientist and geologist.
  Some criticised him for ruining
    the landscape with his heavy
    industrial schemes but in this
  he was typical of the new wave
    of entrepreneurs who were
  reshaping the economy of the land.

There was a ferry which brought
workers from Broseley across the
  river to Coalport. Reynolds soon
  acquired a half share in this
  enterprise and then arranged with
  the ferryman to be transported
    across at any time of the day
    or night. There is a story that
  on one occasion he could not
rouse the boatman in the middle of
the night and, after walking all
    the way round via the bridge,
  he broke every window in his
  cottage but had them all replaced
    the next day.

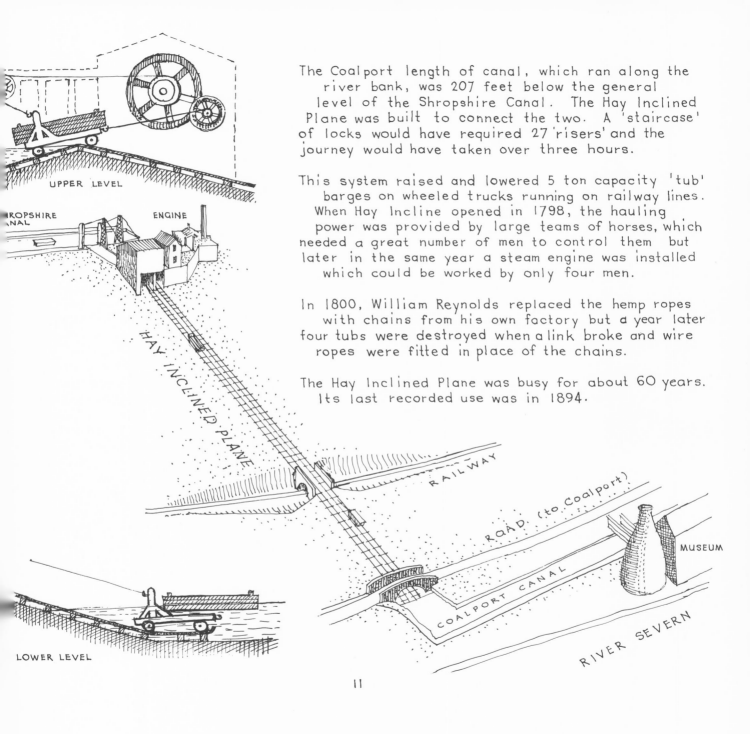

The Coalport length of canal, which ran along the river bank, was 207 feet below the general level of the Shropshire Canal. The Hay Inclined Plane was built to connect the two. A 'staircase' of locks would have required 27 'risers' and the journey would have taken over three hours.

This system raised and lowered 5 ton capacity 'tub' barges on wheeled trucks running on railway lines. When Hay Incline opened in 1798, the hauling power was provided by large teams of horses, which needed a great number of men to control them but later in the same year a steam engine was installed which could be worked by only four men.

In 1800, William Reynolds replaced the hemp ropes with chains from his own factory but a year later four tubs were destroyed when a link broke and wire ropes were fitted in place of the chains.

The Hay Inclined Plane was busy for about 60 years. Its last recorded use was in 1894.

UPPER LEVEL

SHROPSHIRE CANAL   ENGINE

HAY INCLINED PLANE

RAILWAY

ROAD (to Coalport)

COALPORT CANAL

MUSEUM

RIVER SEVERN

LOWER LEVEL

During a foggy night in 1799, with the Severn at flood level,
   the ferry boat between Coalport and Broseley capsized.
28 of the workers from the china factory were drowned. Some
of the bodies were not recovered until 15 months later
   many miles away.

The ferry operated by means of a line from the top of a short
mast fixed to a rock anchor on the river bed. With the bow
   facing upstream, to take advantage of the current, by the
skilful use of the tiller the boat swung from bank to bank.
It relied on good conditions and fine judgement.

After the disaster, various accusations were made – that the
   ferryman was not only new to the job but was also drunk;
that the boat was overloaded, with 43 on board; even that he
had a grievance against some of the passengers, having been
   refused admission to a local dance.

The following morning, a large number of china articles were
   found floating in the calm shallows. They had been stolen
from the works and were concealed in the workers' garments.
Tighter security arrangements were introduced at the factory.

John Rose paid for the coffins of those who were drowned.

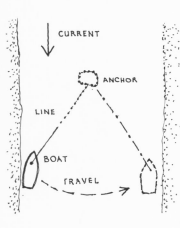

John Wesley made his first visit to the Coalport area in 1764. The parish church at Madeley could not contain the crowds that came to hear him preach and a window was removed for the benefit of those who had to stand out in the yard.

Eighteen years later he returned to help the local Evangelist preacher, John Fletcher, revive the chapel and classes in the community. Fletcher was Swiss and his original surname was de la Flechère. He became one of the extraordinary figures in the religious movement, considered by some to be second only to Wesley himself. With only one short break, due to bad health, he was active in Coalport for twenty years.

Drunkenness was a major social problem and was the concern of employers as well as church leaders. Reynolds and Darby petitioned the magistrates to reduce the number of "tippling houses" in the district from 30 to 18 - even though some of them were owned by Reynolds - but drinking continued and by 1847 the number had increased to 52.

Workers at the China Works used to smuggle bottles of drink into the factory and conceal them by hanging them out of the windows on string into the river.

Hay Farm stood on top of the hill overlooking the China Works. With 266 acres it was the largest holding in the parish. Abraham Darby II bought half of the Hay in 1758 and his son Abraham Darby III, builder of the Iron Bridge, bought the remainder. He lived in the house until his death in 1789. A year earlier he sold 20 acres to his relative and business associate Richard Reynolds, who then leased them to his son William. It was on this land that the Coalport development took place and on which the branch of the Shropshire Canal and Hay Inclined Plane were constructed.

After building the Blakeway and Rose factory, John Rose later bought a further two acres on the other side of the road on which to extend his works and build some workers' cottages. Later still he took up residence in Hay Farm - a perfect spot from which to view his enterprise.

William Reynolds had a financial interest in Bradley's earthenware factory, which occupied the site between the canal and the river bank, but it was not a very successful business, especially after Rose's China Works opened up immediately behind it. Eventually Bradley's was taken over by the larger concern.

In 1803, Blakeway & Rose were declared bankrupt, due to the failure of their banking business. The Works were bought by Cuthbert Johnson and William Clarke. John Rose continued as Manager and the company name was changed to John Rose & Company.

When William Reynolds died in the same year, his cousin Robert Anstice took over his share of Bradley's Pottery and the firm became Anstice, Horton & Rose – Reynolds had taken Thomas Rose, John's brother, into partnership.

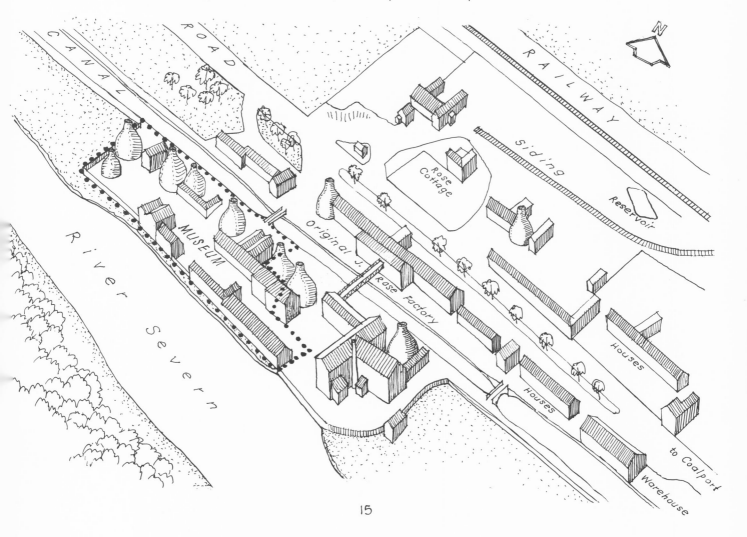

The new firm of John Rose & Company,
which was formed in 1803, was well
managed and financially sound. With
John Rose's technical skill and
great knowledge of the trade it went
from strength to strength.

In 1814, the partnership of Robert
Anstice, William Horton and Thomas
Rose was dissolved. The old Bradley
Pottery was acquired and this
made possible the amalgamation of
the two sets of premises for greater
efficiency.

Production had continued at Caughley
but when the lease ran out two years
later John Rose decided to concentrate
production at Coalport. Kilns and
other equipment were transferred to
increase capacity even further.

The old clock, which had been at the
Caughley factory since the latter part of
the 18th century, was also taken over. It
remained at Coalport until 1926 and is still
preserved at Stoke-on-Trent.

Coalport China Works became one of the
major centres for the production of
fine decorative wares and established
a reputation for quality in the home
market and abroad.

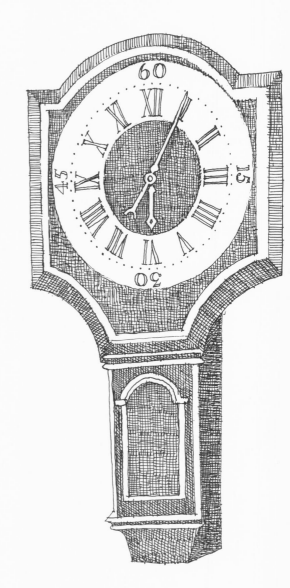

Transfer printing on pottery was probably introduced into England by John Brookes round about 1749-50.

Thomas Turner used the method at Caughley, combining and adapting the ideas of other manufacturers to his own designs. Robert Hancock, an engraver from Worcester, went to work for Turner in 1775 and further refined printing techniques.

Artists were the elite among pottery workers. They received the highest wages and enjoyed the best working conditions. Many of them were allowed to engage in free-lance work for other manufacturers but there was great concern about the copying of popular designs and the disclosure of trade secrets.

The Indian Tree pattern originated from the Coalport China Works in 1801.

Like the Blue Willow it was a classic design which became universally popular and remains so to this day.

Although there are many technicalities and variations, the basic process of manufacture is the same for china and earthenware.

The raw material is clay of a suitable type mixed with special ingredients to give the required characteristics.

Shaping is carried out by moulding, turning, 'throwing' on a wheel or hand-modelling.

The shapes are then 'biscuit' fired to make them hard.

Glazing is applied to give a thin layer of glass, then 'glost' fired, after which decoration is applied before a final firing. In some products the decoration is applied direct to the biscuit.

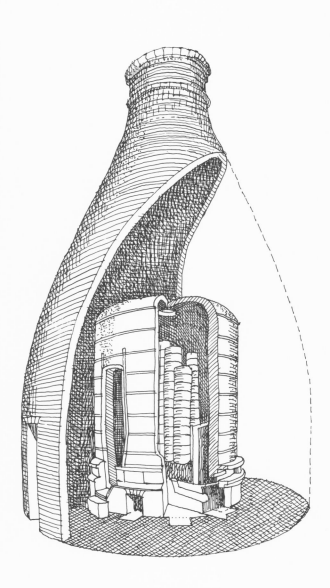

The traditional 'Bottle' kiln – so named because of its shape – was used at the Coalport Works. It consisted of two separate chambers. The outer, called the 'Hovel', was built of brick and swept upwards in a gentle curve to the small circular opening at the top. This was to give a good 'draught' for the fireboxes. The inner chamber was the kiln and was built of fireclay blocks, banded with steel, to withstand temperatures of up to 1250°C, the heat required to 'fire' china.

The shaped pieces were first taken to the Green Room where they were 'cured' (allowed to dry out slowly) to avoid cracking. After examination they were placed in saggars (fireclay containers) and bedded in finely ground flint to support them. To allow for the escape of any steam, from moisture still contained by the wares, the lids were not sealed down. They were then stacked in the kiln.

The 'biscuit' firing took between 42 and 48 hours at temperatures of about 1225 - 50°c This caused a partial fusion of the Silica in the clay and changed its chemical state. This is known as 'vitrification'.

After cleaning and further inspection, the Coalport mark was applied, as approval for the piece to be glazed and decorated.

The 'glost' firing took up to 30 hours at a temperature of about 1100°C. The saggars used for this stage had a glazed lining and the lids were sealed to exclude smoke and dust.

These were intermittent kilns, consisting of a single chamber which remained idle in the periods of loading and unloading. After prolonged periods of intense heat, a considerable time was required for cooling. Demand for maximum production meant that to speed the emptying stage 'biscuit placers'- or labourers - often had to enter the inner chambers at very high temperatures. Added to this, the dust and working hours of up to 14 per day made it an unpleasant and unhealthy occupation.

Arsenic and lead were used in the preparation of glaze and these produced a health
hazard for the 'Dippers' who applied it . They contracted 'Potter's Rot', which
produced eventual paralysis after continual exposure to the poisonous ingredients.
John Rose found a way of excluding these substances and was awarded the Gold
Medal of the Royal Society of Arts for this humanitarian development. With a
shrewd eye for publicity, he introduced a new trade mark proclaiming the award on
30 May 1820.

By introducing pure felspar - then known as felt spar - it was possible to achieve
a product equal to that using pure kaolin - the ingredient which gave the classic
egg-shell finish to Chinese ware. Manufacture was more technically controllable,
economic and healthier.

In the same year that the award was made, John Rose & Company bought out the Swansea
Porcelain Company and the Nantgarw factory, where William Billingsley and Samuel
Walker, his son-in-law, had developed a new kind of kiln. In addition they held a closely
guarded secret recipe for producing a soft paste porcelain which was superior to the
hard paste formula used at Coalport.

Billingsley and Walker, together with their recipe and equipment, were transferred to the Coalport Works and their ideas were incorporated into production methods.

Apart from established commercial lines, a new class of buyer was emerging who could afford the best and wished its value to be obvious. The opulent collection named 'Coalbrookdale' was introduced to meet this demand. Billingsley was an acknowledged master of the new technique of flower modelling and painting.
This Rococco style required an advanced skill and manufacture could only be undertaken after the many technical difficulties had been overcome.

The flowers, with their delicate petals and leaves, were added to the body of the piece and fired at the same time. The item was then glazed and fired. Finally it was painstakingly enamelled by hand before passing through the kiln again.

Some of the pieces went through 50 pairs of hands during manufacture.

John Randall was a geologist and local historian as well as being one of the principal artists at Coalport. His speciality was bird painting. John learned his trade from his uncle, Thomas Martin Randall who was also a painter and engraver for Thomas Turner at Caughley. In later years Thomas started his own factory at Madeley where, after early disasters, he succeeded in making a porcelain closely resembling that manufactured by the world-famous French firm of Sèvres.

Thomas Randall developed the deep turquoise, made possible by the complete amalgamation of the paint and the glaze. He refused to forge the Sèvres mark, even though he was capable of counterfeiting the quality and was employed by the French firm to decorate some of their products.

John Randall was also able to paint in the style and on one occasion was called into the office by John Rose's nephew, who had taken over the firm, shown a piece of china his employer had purchased at high price - as being genuine Sèvres - and asked if he could copy it. John replied that it would be strange if he couldn't as he had painted the original, as a boy, while working for his uncle.

Rock House and Swinney Mill stood close by Coalport Bridge. Water from a stream in the hillside was carried along a wooden channel and discharged into boxes round the rim of a 76 feet diameter 'overshot' wheel which powered the grinding of materials for the China Works.

Until the strike in 1833, cordial relations existed at the factory but John Rose was in dispute with some of his workers, who wished to join a trade union. They had their 'Pitcher' (sick society) and a travelling society to help those seeking employment but as it was no longer a crime to be a trade unionist some wished to join. A number of employees shared Rose's conviction that "those depending on the daily labour of their hands are not in a position to dictate to their employers" and 28 of them issued at their own expense a printed "Address to the Public" dissociating themselves from the strike. There was little support for the strikers and after much suffering during the hard winter those who had not left the industry returned to work. The loyal staff presented an engraved goblet to John Rose as "A tribute of respect to his public and private character and to the uncompromising firmness with which he has recently resisted the demands of an illegal conspiracy".

Copper plate engraving was invented in Germany during the 15th. century. A technique was later developed to use the principle in the decoration of pottery.

Designs were engraved on to flat copper plates in the normal way. Enamel pigments made from a variety of substances (Copper Oxide for green, Cobalt for blue, etc.) were mixed with oil and heated in a pan. The plate itself was warmed, pigment was spread on and the surface completely cleaned with a knife and a corduroy pad, leaving pigment only in the engraved lines. Then specially prepared tissue was laid over the whole plate and both were passed through a press causing the tissue to lift out the pigment from the lines. After cutting to shape and size, the tissue was placed face down on to the piece of pottery and firmly rubbed by hand to transfer the design. Washing in soapy water removed the tissue and the item was ready for firing to fix the decoration.

24

A fine example of the printer's craft was the commemorative design for Matthew Webb, the first man to swim the English Channel. He had been a naval man before becoming a champion swimmer and was always known as 'Captain'. As a young boy he travelled often from his birthplace in Dawley to swim in the Severn and once saved his brother from drowning. Their ancestor was also a Captain but in Marlborough's army. He married the daughter of John Thursfield who founded the Jackfield Pottery which was eventually bought by Blakeway and managed by John Rose. Matthew Webb lost his life in July 1883 attempting to swim the rapids below Niagara Falls.

Not until 1918 did the Education Act forbid the employment of children under the age of 12 years, although the Factory Act of 1847 had gone some way to stop children under the age of eight being employed and requiring a break of thirty minutes after five hours in the 10 hour day then being worked by the over twelves.

Conditions in the potteries were better than the mines and mills but young children worked alongside the adults and were used as motive power for the wheels and jolleys. They had to endure the same unhealthy conditions of damp, dust and heat.

The River, which had served Turner at Caughley for the transport of Cornish clay and finished goods; the canal, which had halved John Rose's costs and given access to wider markets, were both challenged by the railways after 1861.

A Coalport branch of the London & North Western Railway was opened in that year for both passenger and goods traffic.

For many years the little engine, nicknamed 'The Dodger' plied the tracks between Coalport Station and Wellington.

For a while after John Rose died, his brother Thomas and nephew William maintained production and the Company received honours at major exhibitions in London, France and the Chicago World Fair but when William retired in 1862, John Rose & Company almost faded into obscurity and finally a receiver was appointed. About 1885 the Works was bought by Peter Schuyler Bruff and when he was joined by his son Charles, four years later, the business again began to prosper.

Thomas John Bott was appointed Art Director. He had served his apprenticeship at the Royal Worcester China Factory and later held jobs with leading firms in Stoke as a ceramic artist.

With Peter Bruff's capital and business acumen, Charles's drive, imagination and fine sensitivity assisted by Bott's flair and artistic talent the firm expanded. Old favourite designs were revived, the staff were given encouragement and originality fostered. No imitations were permitted. By the time Thomas Bott and Charles Bruff went to the Chicago World Fair of 1893, Coalport China was a success and the name was again highly regarded.

William, Prince of Orange and his Princess visited John Rose's works a year after production began in 1796. The young couple had fled to this country when Holland was invaded by the French Revolutionary troops under Napoleon.

By 1900, when the Duchess of York, Mary, later to be Queen, was seeing the China Works and showroom the old buildings had been modernised and most of the 500 employees of the china Manufactory were in Coalport High Street to welcome the Royal visitor.

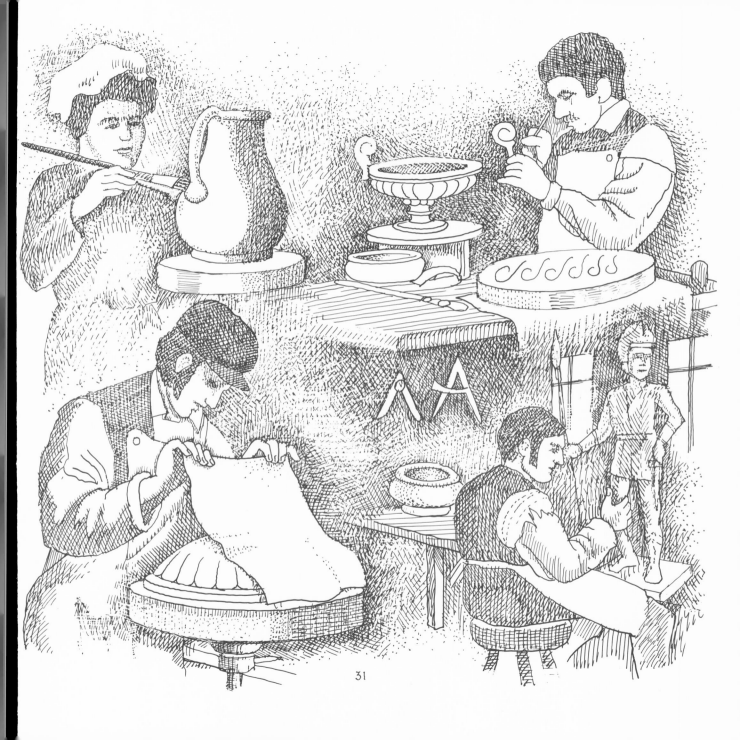

Coalport China Company survived
the First World War, but by
1923, after repeated annual
crises, the struggle became
impossible. When a reduction
in wages was demanded by the
management there was a walk-
out by the workforce which was
quickly recognised by the Union
as an official strike.

The Bruffs, who had updated
and improved manufacturing and
working conditions, were bitterly
disappointed and finally sold
the firm to the Cauldon Pottery
Company, which decided in 1926
to move production to Shelton
in Staffordshire.

During the 19th century the china
and earthenware industry had
become increasingly concentrated
within the Stoke-on-Trent area.
Coalport was relatively isolated
from other companies and the
services, skills and technology
developing there. The move to
'The Potteries' forged connections
with many famous names.

Many of the workpeople travelled
daily from Shropshire to Stoke-
on-Trent; many settled in the area
and it was a long time before the
'Shropshire Brogue' disappeared
from the factory floor.

The Cauldon Pottery was founded early in the 19th century by Job Ridgway, who served his apprenticeship with Wedgwood. The business remained in his family until 1859.

At the time Coalport China moved to Stoke-on-Trent, the firm was controlled by Harold Taylor Robinson and Associates.

Cauldon acquired the name and stock-in-trade and Coalport's established lines continued to be produced.

COALPORT TEA SERVICE
"LADY ANNE" DESIGN

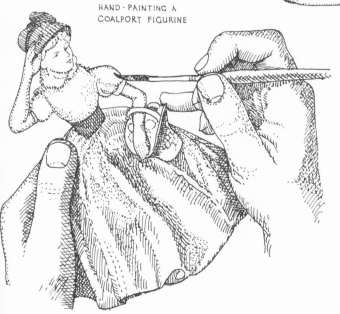

HAND-PAINTING A
COALPORT FIGURINE

Through the links with Cauldon, the techniques of multi-colour transfer printing were obtained from F. & R. Pratt & Co who had previously controlled the Cauldon Earthenware Division where the famous Pratt pot lids were made.

In 1932, the Cauldon Company went into liquidation. The Coalport name survived and was able, through a director of the Company, to buy Cauldon Potteries and production continued at Shelton.

Ten years after the move from Shropshire, further changes occured. The firm was moved to the Crescent Pottery and became part of George Jones & Sons Ltd. Production continued in this factory until 1958, when it was decided that the works were not adequate for post-war production and they were closed down.

OLD FOLEY WORKS

When it was announced that the company which had its origins in a simple works at Caughley and had achieved a world-wide reputation was to close down it attracted the attention of the international press. The name was again taken over and work was transferred to the Foley Works in Fenton, Stoke-on-Trent, which is the site of the present factory. Potting was established at Foley in 1850 by William Robinson & Co. In 1885 the premises were purchased by Mr E. Brain, an energetic man, prominent in public life and widely travelled.

After Mr Brain's death in 1910, the Company was guided to still greater prosperity by his son, Mr W.H. Brain and it was his son, Mr E. William Brain, whose influence led to the re-establishment of the quality and charm of Coalport China after over a quarter of a century of fluctuating fortunes. Many of the famous old patterns were revived; the old art of 'Coalbrookdale' floral encrusted wares was re-introduced and the renowned Pastille Burner Cottage models, reproduced from the original moulds, were available again. Such was his regard for the Coalport name that production of Foley China ceased after 1963 and only Coalport was produced at the Foley Works.

JOHN BROMLEY
FIGURINE AND FAUNA MODELLER

The 1960's saw the development in the British Ceramics Industry of bigger organisations backed by larger resources. Many of the family-owned companies were incorporated into the large groups that were being formed and in 1967 Coalport became a Member of the Wedgwood Group.

The advantages of this connection have been considerable. Coalport maintains its own identity as a manufacturer and is a Member of the Fine Bone China Manufacturers' Association.

The Coalport name is still closely associated with richly decorated prestige items; many produced in limited editions to commemorate special occasions which, with a broad range of tableware and gift products of international appeal, will carry this famous name into the future.

ACKNOWLEDGEMENTS ·

My thanks for assistance to:

Joanna Bickerton
John Powell
Ironbridge Gorge Museum
Shrewsbury Central Library
Bromley Library Service
Coalport China, Stoke
Josiah Wedgwood & Sons Ltd
Alan Hughes
Sheila Wilson

Published works consulted:

Archer H.G.   'Coalport Porcelain'
                 Windsor Magazine 1880
Edmundson R.   'Coalport China Works'
                 Industrial Archeology Review 1978-9
Jewitt L.   'A History of Coalport China Works'
                 The Art Journal 1862
Mackenzie C.   'The House of Coalport 1750-1950'
                 Collins 1951
Randall J.   'Coalport Porcelain Works'
                 History of Madeley 1880
Trinder B.   'The Industrial Revolution in Shropshire'
                 1973 & 1981
Ironbridge Gorge Museum booklets on the area